S0-BXK-020

THE
Irresistible
Church SERIES

Call Me FRIEND

Building Compelling Relationships Through **ONE-ON-ONE MINISTRY**

by Kate Brueck

Call Me Friend
ISBN 978-1-946237-02-6

Author–Kate Brueck
Contributing Author– Marisa Altamirano
Collaborators– Rebecca Staver, Cameryn Bartschi
Contributing Editors– Ali Howard and Mike Dobes
Editor in Chief–Marc Stein

Printed in the United States of America.

Produced by The Denzel Agency (www.denzel.org)
Cover and Interior Design: Rob Williams

For information or to order additional print copies of this and other resources contact:

Joni and Friends International Disability Center
P.O. Box 3333, Agoura Hills, California 91376-3333
Email: churchrelations@joniandfriends.org
Phone: 818-707-5664

Kindle version available at www.irresistiblechurch.org

CONTENTS

Introduction

Buddies. Shadows. Sidekicks. Heroes. Lifeguards. Crew members. Friends. These are all titles worn by volunteers who step into a one-on-one support role for a person with special needs, disability or learning difference in the context of ministry.

No matter what you call it, buddy ministry may very well be the most frequently mentioned special needs ministry model of our time. A buddy ministry is a program of the church designed to support the disability community by pairing an individual with a disability with a buddy during church services so that they can better participate in the mainstream programs of the local church. This is a more inclusive approach than relocating everyone with a disability to a separate classroom or expecting our friends' special needs to disappear when they enter a church building. Buddy ministry can provide the extra support needed to make church a fruitful experience for all involved.

Believing that buddy ministry is an effective answer to the needs of many individuals with special needs and knowing how to organize and implement an effective buddy ministry are two separate matters. It is the nitty-gritty how-tos that leave ministry leaders scratching their heads, wondering if they will ever be able to offer something more than a patched-together emergency response to special needs. Prayerfully, this book will provide the concrete know-how and the confidence to implement your own effective, biblical buddy ministry.

Two Are Better than One

Scripture is full of famous pairs that bring to life the truth stated in Ecclesiastes 4:9 (ESV): "Two are better than one, because they have a good reward for their toil." From Adam and Eve, to David and Jonathan, to Paul and Barnabas, God has often used the combined efforts of two people to multiply ministry for His kingdom. A friend once told me, "If Jesus had sent out the disciples one by one, they maybe could have covered twice as much ground, but He sent them out two by two. That seems to be the model of Scripture; it's not every man for himself. We are connected. 'As iron sharpens iron, so one man sharpens another' (Proverbs 27:17)."

Let's take a closer look at one of these famous pairs: Moses and Aaron. In the life of the modern church, this pair provides a beautiful example of godly partnership and "sharpening" that can be applied to special needs buddy ministry.

In Exodus chapters 3–4, Moses was keeping sheep at Mount Horeb when he saw a bush that was on fire without being consumed. As Moses approached the bush, God spoke to him instructing him to lead the Hebrews out of Egypt. God gave him several signs and wonders to help him accomplish this great task, but Moses declined, saying, "Oh, my Lord, I am not eloquent, either in the past or since you have spoken to your servant, but I am slow of speech and of tongue" (Exodus 4:10). He and God argued a bit, and in the end God said, "Is there not Aaron, your brother, the Levite? I know that he can speak well. Behold, he is coming out to meet you, and when he sees you, he will be glad in his heart. You shall speak to him and put the words in his mouth, and I will be with your mouth and with his mouth and will teach you both what to do."

Moses believed his disability, a speech impediment of some kind, disqualified him from serving God. However, God made it clear that Moses, with his limitations, was the one chosen to accomplish this task.

Graciously, God also gave Moses what we could call a "buddy" in his brother Aaron. An older guy who could speak well, Aaron provided the human support Moses felt he needed to accomplish this grand call on his life. Aaron demonstrates the attitude of an effective buddy in how he responded: "he was glad in his heart" when he saw Moses. In addition, God promised to be with both Moses and Aaron and teach them both what to do. What a great example of a buddy ministry!

An Irresistible Vision

Just as Aaron provided the confidence and support Moses needed to complete his calling, so too buddies provide encouragement and assistance to friends[1] of all ages in a church community so that they can be fully involved in Kingdom life. This starts with the opportunity to know and respond to the good news of Jesus Christ. God has called the Church to share the gospel with all people. Thankfully, Scripture also makes it clear that saving faith comes from the power of the Word—not from our intellectual abilities or social skill: "So faith comes from hearing, and hearing through the word of Christ" (Romans 10:17).

Believing that Christ lived a perfect life, believing that He died for one's sins and rose again to reign for all eternity, repenting of sin, and submitting to His rule are not where the Christian life ends; these are where it is born. The Holy Spirit then begins to mold and shape the Christian to look and act more like Jesus as he or she grows in grace. This process works best when done in conjunction with discipleship—learning from other Christians what it means to be a Christian. Perhaps one of the clearest and most familiar passages of Scripture relating to this process is the Great Commission. Jesus says, "Go therefore and make disciples of all nations, baptizing them in the name of the Father and of the Son and of the Holy Spirit, teaching them to observe all that I have commanded you" (Matthew 28:19-20a). As believers, we are instructed to make disciples by teaching them all that Jesus taught. This new life involves worship, service, fellowship and growth in faith.

You may be thinking, *Why make such a point of reviewing the foundations of the Christian life when starting a discussion on buddy ministry?* I believe that without these basics firmly in place, we may structure a very important ministry on the wrong motivations.

For example, you might implement a buddy ministry out of a desire for parents to be able to attend service together instead of taking turns on Sunday mornings. This is valid and admirable, but it does not go far enough. Without proper vision for evangelism and discipleship of *all* people, this endeavor may still be a blessing to parents, but it could turn into nothing more than a babysitting situation for the child.

An equally unsatisfying motivation is focusing purely on outreach. A church may desire to reach the special needs community and put together a spectacular plan for making sure families can attend church. The danger is that when there is a slow response, the church discontinues the ministry, believing the outreach plan has failed and it is not worth the effort to provide buddies for one or two people. Because the motivation was based on numbers, not on discipleship, the church misses a prime opportunity to build the Kingdom one family, or one person, at a time.

Holding firm the understanding that ministry of any type is ultimately about evangelism and discipleship will help a local church avoid shipwrecking ministry efforts on wrong motivations. Unashamedly demonstrating this belief through special needs ministry screams to a world that places unbalanced value on social skills, intellect, and power that our God really does love us because of who He is, not because of who we are or what we have done. This places the spotlight on our irresistible Savior, and suddenly, His Church becomes irresistible as we live this out—whether in the life of one family or one hundred families.

Note

1. Within the context of this book, *buddy* is the name we have given to those who serve within special needs ministry, and *friend* is the name we have given to individuals who are served by the special needs ministry.

What Buddies Provide

Below we have compiled many components of what a buddy can provide to a friend with special needs. A good buddy does not need to simultaneously exhibit all of these qualities independently but should strive to work with other volunteers and leaders to incorporate as many of these components as possible in the life of his or her friend.

A Buddy Provides Discipleship

Once we understand that the ultimate purpose of buddy ministry is evangelism and discipleship, the qualification for a good buddy becomes fairly simple. A good buddy is someone who exhibits the fruit of the Spirit because his or her life has been transformed by the redeeming power of Jesus Christ. This means that for one disciple to make another disciple, demonstrating God's love, joy, peace, patience, kindness, goodness, gentleness, faithfulness and self-control is more important than having a degree in special education (see Galatians 5:22-23a). Buddies can work alongside the classroom teacher to communicate the gospel and take their friends deeper in the Word.

Along with personally experiencing the work of the Holy Spirit, a buddy must believe that the Holy Spirit can work in others' lives, regardless of their apparent abilities or disabilities. Signing up to work with a person one on one, without truly believing that person can have saving faith, a place of service, or any depth of Christian understanding, is a recipe for babysitting rather than discipleship.

Amy's Story

Ronda runs a strong special needs ministry in her church, but you would never have found her considering special needs ministry before her daughter, Amy, became a Christian. Ronda and her husband adopted Amy and incorporated her into the life of their family, including church, cheerleading and travel. But Ronda did not believe Amy was able to express faith in Jesus because of her severe disabilities, including being nonverbal. Ronda brought Amy to church simply so Amy could be with the family.

At one evening service, the pastor closed his sermon with a clear gospel call and invited those who wanted to accept Christ as their Savior to come to the altar at the front. Amy placed her mother's hands on her wheelchair and pointed to the altar. Ronda felt that Amy could not understand the call and therefore ignored her, believing Amy was just trying to follow the crowd. Amy continued to make it clear that she wished to go to the front of the church. Finally, to keep Amy calm, Ronda pushed her down the aisle and waited with her. At the altar, Amy cried and seemed to pray for several minutes. When finished, her face radiated with peace and joy. Ronda realized she had just witnessed her daughter giving her life to Christ.

Ronda also realized that she had been wrong to assume that Amy had a free pass to heaven simply because she had special needs and could not communicate her faith openly. From that moment, Ronda committed to sharing the love of Jesus with the special needs community and to allowing God to work instead of picking and choosing who *she* thought God could reach. Ronda finally understood that the Holy Spirit speaks everyone's language.

A Buddy Provides Friendship

Remember how God noted that Aaron would be glad in his heart when he saw Moses? Aaron was not focused on Moses' disability—he was focused on Moses as a person, and he apparently really liked him! Good buddies get to know the individual they are paired with as a person. They discover what they have in common and what they can learn from the other person. They might develop a relationship that has inside jokes, favorite activities, and shared experiences. They enjoy spending time together. In other words, they become friends.

A person does not have to be able to communicate, be self-sufficient, or even respond to outside stimuli to be worth spending time with. Simply because a person is created in the image of God makes being together a valuable and enjoyable use of time. A traditional give-and-take friendship may not be possible at first glance; but, by investing time and energy into their friend, I believe buddies will find they look forward to being together and miss their friends when they are unable to meet. These are true marks of friendship. For compelling insight on building a life-giving friendship with someone affected by disability, check out Henri Nouwen's book, *Adam*.

Providing friendship in Christian community does not mean the buddy should be available around the clock or suddenly become inseparable from the family he or she serves. By clearly defining a buddy's terms of service and working as a ministry team, you protect your volunteers from being bombarded with requests for free babysitting, from fielding phone calls at all times of the day and night, or from being expected to shift service without notice. In my experience, these issues are few and far between as the vast majority of families served by buddy ministry would never dream of taking advantage of someone who is providing such a valuable blessing.

With the expectations for service clearly defined from the beginning, many buddies find that they still enjoy personally supporting their friend along with their family outside of church in a variety of ways. Attending a Special Olympics competition, a birthday party, a school performance, or another community event in which their friend is participating is a great way to solidify friendship and show support. Simply sharing an experience together, such as attending a baseball game, visiting a museum, or inviting the family to a party, is another great way to get to know each other and provide friendship.

If a buddy chooses to invest extra time outside of church, it can actually provide the buddy with incredible insight into how to best serve his friend during the scheduled program times. Watching his friend compete on a sports team or spending time with his friend's family is a great way to learn new avenues for communication, new areas of common ground, and new skills he might not have known existed. Because of these benefits, some churches choose to write into their buddy position descriptions that the buddy will participate in their friend's life outside of church at least once a quarter.

A buddy can help her friend build relationships with her friend's peers and other volunteers within the church as well. In doing so a buddy contributes toward building a community where everyone fully belongs.

Buddies, along with the classroom leadership and other volunteers, also provide a level of friendship with the entire family they serve. It is extremely helpful for buddies and leadership to recognize that the caregivers are the experts on the friends in their class and to seek to support the vision the family has for their loved one. Often the caregivers are parents of a child, teen, or

This symbol indicates that there are supplemental resources that correspond with this topic at http://www.joniandfriends.org/church-relations/

adult with special needs, but a caregiver could also be a spouse, sibling, legal guardian, or paid health worker. Regardless of the home situation, the buddy and classroom leadership should strive to maintain a positive and complementary relationship with those providing full-time care. Siblings are often neglected in the conversation surrounding special needs ministry, but they are frequently just as concerned as their parents about good care and community for their brother or sister with special needs. Getting to know the whole family is a great way to serve all members of the family.

Finally, a true friend prays for his or her friends. We encourage you to incorporate regular prayer into your ministry. Set aside time as a team to pray for the spiritual development of your friends, as well as for their health and well-being and that of their families.

A Buddy Helps Provide Safety

Safety is of paramount importance in any ministry. Physical safety from environmental harm, whether due to emergency situations or to the malicious intentions of other people, should factor into how we do ministry at any level. Safety concerns within special needs ministry certainly requires forethought and practical arrangements from leadership to volunteers, but this should not scare the local church away from buddy ministry. Instead, buddy ministry can be wholeheartedly embraced as a very successful answer to how to keep our most vulnerable church members safe.

According to a 2012 study published in the journal *Pediatrics*, 46% of children ages 4-7 and 27% of children ages 8-11 who have autism wander away from or bolt from safe places.[1] These numbers are significantly higher than their typical peers' propensity toward elopement. If you have students in your children's ministry with autism, pairing them with a buddy who is responsible for sticking with them is an effective safety measure.

Perhaps less common but just as harmful, additional safety issues can include self-injurious behavior, environmental allergens, and physical environments that endanger a person with limited mobility. Self-injurious behavior might be a friend biting her own hands or picking at her skin until she bleeds as a result of anxiety or sensory overload. It is invaluable to have a buddy on hand to teach the friend who is experiencing distress more appropriate coping behaviors, such as deep breathing or squeezing a stress ball. Checking with the caregivers of friends who exhibit self-injurious behavior can help buddies and classroom leadership reinforce any behavior modification plan already in place. A buddy can also help his friend steer clear of snacks to which the friend is allergic, including items volunteers know not to provide but other classroom participants might try to share unaware. For multi-story buildings, your leadership and buddies can be trained in your church's evacuation procedures to ensure a wheelchair user or person with limited mobility gets downstairs and out of the building when the elevators are out of commission.

Research suggests that people with special needs are roughly three times more likely to be sexually abused as their typical counterparts.[2] It is imperative that the church have airtight procedures to protect participants from this danger. Having a clean background check and personal history on each volunteer is a good first step in providing a safe environment. Check with your church leadership to see what kind of background check procedures they may already have in place for their children's ministry. No person with special needs should ever be left alone with just one other person, no matter how trustworthy that person may seem. Keeping doors open and having multiple adults present can prevent a volunteer with immoral inclinations from having the opportunity to act improperly. For all participants, especially for individuals who have no communication or limited communication skills, this policy should be nonnegotiable.

While not as glaring as immediate physical safety, a buddy can also help provide social and emotional safety. Helping a child, teen, or adult navigate group situations, social pressures, and conversations with others can smooth the way to true friendships and can help avoid bullying.

A Buddy Provides Participation

Use your imagination to compare a class of students to the inner workings of an old-fashioned clock. Each member is a gear that fits into the whole. No member sits alone, spinning away without interacting with the others. Often, however, this kind of interconnected social environment takes some extra support for the student who does not naturally interact with others.

Enter buddy ministry.

The goal is for each of our friends to participate as fully as he or she can—both in the activities of the day and in the social opportunities created by the group environment. The danger is to confuse supporting someone else's participation with participating for them. An example of participating for someone would be to make picture-perfect crafts for your friend with special needs as opposed to encouraging and equipping her to make her own unique craft. Running the relay race or saying the Bible verse in place of your assigned friend is also participating for her.

A good buddy works hard to help her friend participate to her friend's utmost potential by encouraging her to engage. The buddy may provide hands-on assistance for a craft, but she should ask her friend what she would like done next and what she wants it to look like. A buddy may need to help fill in words in a Bible verse, but she should try many different ways to have her friend demonstrate her knowledge of the verse on her own. Demonstrating this knowledge could include hand motions, using picture cards to relate the concepts of the verse, or singing a song together.

It is important for your ministry team to understand that everyone has his or her limits with certain activities. I personally do not enjoy playing volleyball at all. Being forced to join a game of volleyball is a sure way to ruin that portion of my day. And while team activities can sometimes be helpful in discipleship, I am not missing out on the love of Jesus by sitting out or by keeping score. A well-trained buddy and ministry team pay attention to which activities are total killjoys and then help their friends either find something useful in it or find something else to do. In other words, we all have things we love to do and things we hate to do. Avoid forcing someone to do something inconsequential they absolutely despise simply because they have special needs and we want them to participate in everything possible. Understand that everyone has a unique personality with likes and dislikes as he or she was created by God, and those with special needs are no exception.

A buddy is invaluable in helping his friend participate in planned activities because he can help assess how much is too much. If one of your friends with autism is overwhelmed by the praise and worship time, his buddy can provide another activity during worship that is not overwhelming. Perhaps giving thanks in prayer or reading psalms of praise together in a quiet location can fulfill the same purpose without sending the friend into sensory overload. A buddy may work with leadership and other volunteers to gradually ease his friend into other activities over several weeks. Maybe during the first few weeks, his friend can successfully worship with one song, but then he needs to leave. A few weeks later, his friend might have worked up to singing two songs, and so on. Having buddies in the classroom helps provide the liberty and safety to make those decisions on the fly.

A buddy also provides the freedom for a friend to participate in unconventional ways. For instance, a friend who has trouble focusing without movement may need the freedom to stand or even pace within a certain part of the classroom in order to pay attention. Others may need to listen to the Bible story from the comfort of a darkened tent that blocks out other distractions. Buddies and classroom leaders can keep track of what is helpful and what is not so that your friends can participate as much as possible in every aspect of Sunday school.

A Buddy Provides Communication Assistance

Buddies help their friends communicate with others. Often kids, teens, and adults with special needs will have unique communication barriers and unique ways of crossing those barriers. Buddies can facilitate communication by helping their friend be heard. When we listen, we communicate to our friends that they are important. Communication is the cornerstone on which we build friendships.

Leadership to Friend

Classroom leaders should be mindful to present each lesson in a way that is accessible to all the children in their classroom. Using visual schedules and interactive lesson plans will help engage individuals with special needs. It is also wise to avoid abstract concepts as many of your friends are likely concrete thinkers. Imagine having a very literal mind and difficulty understanding figures of speech. Now imagine being told that you are "covered in the blood Jesus" or that you need to "ask Jesus into your heart" because "your heart is sick with sin."[3]

If further clarification or explanation is needed beyond what the teacher is providing, a buddy can help his friend deepen his understanding of the lesson. By rewording instructions or reminding his friend of the next step, a buddy can help his friend engage more fully in the Sunday school lesson.

For more information on how your ministry team and buddies can adapt curriculum for your friends, check out the online appendices.

Friend to Leadership and Peers

Buddies can also help classroom leaders and students in the class learn how to communicate with their friend. For example, a buddy might introduce his friend Timmy by sharing that Timmy can't communicate using words, but that he loves it when people give him fist bumps. The buddy might model this and encourage others to greet Timmy in the same way. After doing this for a few weeks, other classroom participants and volunteers can say hi and fist-bump Timmy on their own. A buddy might also help other volunteers, such as worship leaders, small-group leaders, and classroom teachers, understand what his friend is communicating. For example, perhaps your friend uses sign language for requests such as using the restroom or getting water, or to indicate they are upset. Caregivers can teach your ministry team the basic vocabulary of their loved one. With this knowledge, a buddy can help communicate his friend's intentions to other volunteers who may not have consistent exposure to this type of communication.

Friend to Friend

Particularly as your friends transition from children's ministry into youth group, and then become young adults, a buddy's help navigating the social scene can be invaluable. A buddy can gently assist her friend into and out of conversations. A buddy, along with ministry leadership, can help her friend navigate boy-girl relationships appropriately as the friend ages. For all ages, a buddy can also help diffuse situations in which her friend has become offended by or has upset another person. Particularly for friends who exhibit impulsive behaviors, having a buddy reinforce clear social and physical boundaries set by your ministry team can prevent a lot of grief and can help facilitate friendship.

To Parents

Parents everywhere ask their child one question when they pick them up from Sunday school, children's church, or youth group: "What did you learn today?" For your nonverbal friends, or those who rarely communicate outside of felt needs, having your ministry team on hand to help answer that question can be a huge blessing. Handing over completed crafts, sharing the Bible lesson, and cluing the parents in to important events are helpful ways a buddy can serve.

A particularly effective tool to communicate your friends' growth in their relationship with Christ is a spiritual journey notebook – a notebook filled with photos and descriptions of important events, like a time they successfully memorized a favorite Bible verse, or the day they were baptized. Allow your creativity to explore what this notebook might look like! Your ministry leadership and buddies can work together to compile this notebook by taking pictures of your friends as they participate in church life. Adding favorite Bible verses or worship song lyrics along with meaningful dates is helpful. Putting this kind of information in a scrapbook throughout the year with short descriptions allows your friends to have a record of belonging and growth that they can share with their families and cherish as a personal testimony.

Many families, particularly those who have children with "invisible" disabilities like autism and ADHD, have been previously dumbfounded by being told upon retrieving their child from class that they are no longer welcome to attend because of behavior issues. Implementing a buddy system can help alleviate the fear that this will happen in your church. If issues do arise that need to be addressed, a buddy can aid leadership in addressing the issue with parents. Having a support system for your friends and their families is instrumental in allowing difficult conversations to be a positive experience rather than an emotionally destructive one.

The Most Important Communication

Ultimately, the buddy, along with your entire ministry team, communicates God's unfailing, all-encompassing, unconditional love for their friend. In the fun times, the hard times, the frightening times, and everything in between, buddies have the opportunity to demonstrate God's great love by their consistency, their character, and their own love. By clearly communicating God's love to his or her friend, the buddy communicates God's love to an entire family.

Lisa's Story

Before Lisa and her husband received the diagnosis of autism for their first-born son, when he was still a toddler, he had difficulty sitting still or participating in his Sunday school class each week. Routinely, about 20 minutes into the pastor's sermon, Lisa would be called to the Sunday school room to assist her son. Lisa never complained about the constant interruption in her spiritual life because she knew her son would be happier with her than struggling in class.

One Sunday, the pattern changed. As Lisa turned the corner to the children's wing, she could hear her son screaming–not defiantly, not squealing with delight, but screaming in terror. Lisa worried that he had been seriously injured as she rushed into his classroom, only to be informed that her son had been removed and was down the hall. She found him in a classroom being held firmly in a chair by an older gentleman. Her son's face radiated terror at being confined. Upon questioning the volunteer, Lisa learned that her son had not harmed another child, been defiant, or been a danger to himself; he simply hadn't been able to settle down that morning.

Lisa picked up her son with a broken heart, feeling that here, in the one place her family had always been accepted, they were no longer welcome. Staying involved in church became a challenge as they felt no one understood or cared about their needs as a family. They began to drift away.

Thankfully, God had a different plan: Tim and Molly. These two volunteers approached Lisa and asked her to bring her son back to Sunday school. Although she initially refused, she finally gave in to their persistent invitations and decided to give it another try, despite her hesitations. Week after week, Tim and Molly seemed happy to see Lisa and her family when they dropped off their son. And week after week, they were still smiling when she picked him up. They always told Lisa at least one thing her son had done well that week, such as sitting quietly during prayer time or participating in the singing. They never told her he was a problem or that his behavior was disruptive. Instead they said, "Please bring your son again next week. We really love spending time with him!"

Because of Tim and Molly's service as buddies, they were able to share the love of Christ with a hurting family.

A Buddy Helps Provide Positive Reinforcement to Shape Behavior

Everyone uses behavior to communicate–a hug, a smile, a scowl, a shoulder shrug. Individuals who struggle to use words rely more heavily on behavior to communicate their desires. Understanding that all behavior is ultimately communication will aid buddies and classroom leadership as they build relationships with their friends.

We encourage you to connect with the parents and caregivers of your friends because they are an invaluable source of information on what makes their loved ones tick. Many buddies will discover that there is already a working behavior management system in place that they can continue during their time together at church. Potential buddies are often worried that they will fail their assigned family in this particular regard. Remembering that the majority of special needs families were not trained to understand their loved one's diagnosis before they received it will be helpful. Buddies should not be worried about becoming a special needs expert. Instead, they should focus their knowledge and energy on becoming an expert on one person with special needs, just like families do.

Behavior management is a component of buddy ministry that will produce a tremendously positive impact. Most volunteers who help lead Sunday school, youth group, children's church, small groups, or other ministries may feel helpless and unequipped when they encounter a student whose behavior they cannot understand. Training your buddies, leadership, and other volunteers to appropriately understand behavior as communication will allow your team to better support your friends and adequately address behavior issues.

Behavior as Communication

To help your team understand behaviors and better interpret the motivations behind behaviors, the acrostic SEAT can be used. It is a great practice to train buddies and other volunteers to think about these four potential categories or functions of behavior. Analyzing each category in light of what you know about your friend, what happened right before his or her behavior was manifested, and what your friend believed was coming next can be critical in understanding what your friend is striving to communicate. Depending on how you and your team choose to handle any given behavior will either reinforce those behaviors or help teach your friends preferred behaviors.

S stands for sensory. This type of behavior generally communicates a preferred sensory experience, whether it is sensory-seeking behavior or sensory-limiting behavior, often referred to as "stimming."

Stimming is repetitive behavior using sounds, physical movement, or movement of objects. This kind of behavior is very common among individuals with autism. Sensory behavior can have many different manifestations, and if the behavior is not disruptive you may choose to allow it. Remember, though, that the ultimate goal is to help your friends engage. If your friends become focused on stimming for too long, you could try to redirect them by using a "first/then" prompt. For example, you could say to them, "*First*, let's sit in the story time circle for three minutes, and *then* you can run."

E stands for escape. This category of behavior communicates a desire to get away from or get out of an undesired activity or situation. A friend may manifest unexpected behaviors to escape something she doesn't like or something that scares her. Perhaps your lesson plan includes reading verses out loud, but this is very intimidating for a friend with a learning disability. To include this friend in the activity, consider having her act out motions for the verse rather than reading one out loud. Another example might be that one of your friends has sensory sensitivity and the volume of the worship music is uncomfortable for him. He may display behavior that indicates a discomfort with worship. In order for him to be included in this church activity, consider providing sound limiting headphones for him or allowing him to worship from the hallway with his buddy where the volume is lower. If an individual melts down at a certain point each week, pause to consider what he or she is trying to communicate and then actively work to modify that activity so that your friend can participate as much as possible.

A stands for attention. This function of behavior communicates a desire to engage someone's attention. Your friends with special needs might use behavior to capture your attention and communicate a desire to interact. Consider what it might look like for a friend who is nonverbal to approach her buddy and communicate her desire to play a game together. Perhaps this friend would approach her buddy, grab the buddy's hand, and begin pulling her in the desired direction. You and your team can begin to teach this friend a preferred behavior by encouraging her to use a visual icon board to express her desire rather than pulling her buddy.

***T* stands for tangibles.** This category of behavior communicates a desire for access to a preferred item or activity. For example, a friend may know that if he continues to make loud noises, he will be given access to a favorite item, such as an iPad, headphones, or stuffed animal. This student may continue displaying this behavior until he receives the favored item. In this scenario, your leadership team or the buddy assigned to this friend might teach their friend a replacement behavior by coaching him to ask nicely for the favored item first. If your friend asks nicely, then reinforce the behavior by saying, “Thank you for asking nicely!” and giving him the favored item. Once your friend masters the concept of asking nicely to gain access to his favored item, the leadership team and his assigned buddy can help him grow further by implementing a “first/then” prompt. Perhaps the buddy might say to his friend, “Great job asking! *First*, let’s do one worship song, and *then* you can have the iPad.” As time progresses, your friend will learn to replace his loud noises with a behavior that is more desirable in order to gain access to his favorite item.

As your friends engage with their peers and others in the Sunday school classroom, remember that all behavior is communication. To learn more about behavior modification, check out the online appendices for this book.

Scheduling

Communicating and maintaining a clear schedule of activities throughout the course of your time together are critical components to a successful buddy ministry. Buddies can help communicate the schedule, with transitions, to their friends to ensure there are no surprises. Particularly for friends on the autism spectrum, a precise schedule can be the difference between hating church and thriving at church. A buddy can use a variety of tools to communicate a schedule, including the following:

- Personal Schedule Checklists—A personal schedule checklist can be kept with the student and marked off as activities are completed. The schedule can be communicated through pictures and/or words.
- First/Then Supports—These are pictures or words that communicate what is happening now and what will happen immediately after. These can be constantly updated throughout the programming.
- Classroom Schedule—A classroom schedule, often an icon schedule with pictures, is something the class follows as a whole and is led by the lead volunteer or teacher.

- Disappearing Timers–Timers, disappearing clocks, etc., are timers that count down to zero and can be used to transition friends from one activity to another without a surprise. Being upfront and consistent about when activities change is key. For example, giving a five-minute warning, a two-minute warning, a one-minute warning, and then removing the activity right on time keeps students grounded in the schedule.

Notes

1. http://www.kennedykrieger.org/overview/news/nearly-half-children-autism-wander-or-%E2%80%9Cbolt%E2%80%9D-safe-places
2. http://www.vera.org/sites/default/files/resources/downloads/sexual-abuse-of-children-with-disabilities-national-snapshot.pdf
3. Barbara Newman, *Autism and Your Church: Nurturing the Spiritual Growth of People with Autism Spectrum Disorder* (Faith Alive Christian Resources, 2011).

Organization: Behind the Scenes

Hopefully by this point, you have discerned whether or not your ministry would benefit from implementing a buddy system. If the answer is yes, you are ready to organize a buddy ministry that meets the needs of your families and volunteers while maintaining the integrity of your church's existing policies and procedures.

Ministry Leadership

A responsible point person for buddy ministry is absolutely imperative to the success and longevity of the ministry. Often, the person who initially handles the behind-the-scenes work is the director or pastor of children's ministry. Routinely, these leaders discover very quickly that adding buddy ministry to their job description gives them an extra part-time job they simply do not have time to do well. To avoid this roadblock, a staff member or lead volunteer with dedicated time needs the support to make this ministry his or her top priority.

Having a point person, often called the Buddy Ministry Coordinator, is helpful for three groups of people: church leadership, volunteers, and families. This Buddy Ministry Coordinator intersects with all three groups of people on a regular basis and ensures that everyone is working on the same team for the same goal. The coordinator receives direction for vision, policy and procedures from leadership. In return, the coordinator keeps leadership informed of family needs, of new ideas and changes that need to take place, and most important, of how God is working through the buddy ministry. The coordinator can also encourage the caretakers to get involved in other ministries in the church that match their gifts and talents. The coordinator helps recruit, train, and keep track of volunteers, including their needs and their service. The coordinator also maintains relationships with the families that utilize the buddy ministry, keeping all intake information up to date and helping to shape individual discipleship and behavior management plans. The coordinator is the person with whom the family communicates their program participation, absences, emergencies, and concerns. With this structure, the Buddy Ministry Coordinator becomes the hub of a special needs ministry wheel. Each spoke of the wheel then knows exactly with whom to coordinate. For a sample job description of the Buddy Ministry Coordinator, visit the online appendices. As your ministry grows, the Buddy Ministry Coordinator will likely need to recruit a leadership team and delegate responsibility. Establishing a leadership team rather than placing full responsibility on one person alone generally allows the ministry to thrive with greater longevity and sustainability.

Chain of Communication

Establishing a Buddy Ministry Coordinator provides a point person for communication between volunteers, families, and church leadership. Because every church is unique, we recommend referring to the general chain of communication set up among the other ministries of your church as a pattern for your ministry. How this communication system looks can vary widely, but having one in place will aid in maintaining calm and order as you serve your friends and their families.

For everyday special needs questions and support, the buddy, the lead teacher, and any other volunteers can troubleshoot with the aid of the Buddy Ministry Coordinator. This helps prevent friends from getting stuck in a vortex of volunteers who are not sure how to help them move forward. It also prevents volunteers from becoming frustrated and giving up because they do not know who to ask for help.

Documentation and Debrief

As with any ministry that requires a community of people to be up to date and able to work together, effective buddy ministry requires documentation to keep moving forward. Instead of keeping pertinent information in the ministry leader's head, keeping a visual and easily accessible record of up-to-date information ensures that if something should suddenly occur to require a change in leadership, the ministry would not suffer.

Proper documentation starts with an intake form, which is sometimes called a ministry profile. This document provides a baseline for understanding your friends' personalities, special needs, correct program placements, spiritual development, dreams, and past experiences. Many excellent intake forms for buddy ministry already exist and can be tweaked to match the needs of your church's ministry structure. However, because needs, abilities, and desires often change with time, this information should be updated on a regular basis, perhaps at the beginning of each year.

If more than one buddy serves a friend over a period of time, keeping a log or journal of what works and what does not can be incredibly helpful. Recording struggles and successes as they occur, along with what triggered them, can help other volunteers navigate those situations. For buddies who serve every other week, being able to check the notes from the previous week means their friend can continue growing in participation instead of having to repeat challenging situations two weeks in a row simply because no one informed the alternating buddy of what happened the week before. Recording positive steps in discipleship and what contributed to them is just as important. For instance, a friend has been working toward praying out loud, and she does so during youth group for the first time; writing down the event and what made it possible will be encouraging and helpful information in the future.

Consider keeping a three-ring binder or file on each person who is being served in the buddy ministry that contains all of the information collected and recorded for the ministry. These should be for internal ministry use only and stored in a safe location where only select individuals have access to the information. Confidentiality is supremely important for the safety of the friend served, the comfort of the family, and the credibility of the ministry. A locked closet, office, filing cabinet, or cupboard can all serve as a safe place for keeping information. This information can also be kept digitally if password protected.

A comprehensive notebook or file could contain the following:

- Up-to-date intake form
- Recent photograph
- Behavior management plan (established by the parents or caregivers)
- Week-to-week log/journal
- Discipleship plan and goals
- A record of spiritual milestones reached

Beyond Buddy Ministry

While buddy ministry can provide an answer to the question of how to fully include individuals in the life of your church, you may encounter students of any age who need more specialized support to thrive. This kind of support can be provided through a self-contained learning environment or a hybrid between self-contained and mainstreamed. To find out more about these options, check out *Pathways to Belonging* in the Joni and Friends Irresistible Church collection.

Organization: On the Front Lines

Having the structure in place behind the scenes is essential, but it is only half the equation. Recruiting, training, scheduling, and supporting the actual buddies are what gives the ministry hands and feet!

Terms of Service

To have a buddy ministry, you must have buddies. These volunteers do not need to have any experience with special needs, but they should be able to offer, with training and support, what was laid out in the section "What Buddies Provide." To recruit these volunteers, it is helpful to have a volunteer job description that can be easily communicated. This description should include the basic expectations, including the period of service, the expected on-duty times, the frequency of service, the place of duty, and to whom they will report. This will help volunteers understand if they can truly commit. It also lets them know that service is manageable and will not prevent them from participating in other church programs.

Some churches have initially arranged their ministry as an on-call, as-needed offering, but we have found that this model simply does not work long-term. It is too difficult to build relationships and provide the structure and consistency needed for our friends with special needs. On-call or as-needed buddy ministries can make the families feel like they are a burden because people are being pulled out of their own programming at the last minute to come and serve their family member. Sundays can already be hard, and when deciding whether or not to make the trek to church, a family might simply opt out without a dedicated buddy waiting for them.

Assigning buddies in pairs to a friend with special needs for a specified length of time allows personal friendship and continuity. These buddies serve every other week, allowing them to participate in other ministries or attend the main service on the alternate weeks. Everyone needs a few weekends to travel or be sick throughout the year as well, and having two buddies who alternate weeks allows these absences to happen naturally without disrupting the ministry.

Additionally, a third person who can serve as a substitute in the case of an emergency or in a month that has a fifth Sunday is a smart addition to the team.

Most ministry leaders first consider using buddies during the worship hour or Sunday school, which traditionally happen on Sunday mornings, and rightfully so, as this is the greatest block of time that families request this ministry. However, don't let that limit your creativity. Buddies can be game-changers for youth group, adult Bible study, Awana clubs, children's choirs and sports teams, and for once-in-a-while events like retreats and respite functions. Just be sure that you try to have a wide base of volunteers so that the same people are not "buddying up" every single time they enter church property.

Recruiting Buddies

Churches are often concerned they will not have enough volunteers to create buddy teams, but there are several ways to help fill the ranks.

First, prayer for great volunteers should be constant. As we have already noted, God is about all people having the opportunity to respond to the gospel and to be discipled. Ask Him for the right volunteers, and continue to ask for His wisdom as you pair buddies with friends.

Second, communicate the need in a variety of venues and ways. Having your lead pastor explain the vision, the need, and how to respond from the pulpit is a great start. Talking to groups of people such as Sunday school classes, small groups, and committees can make a big impact. Sharing personal testimonies from families and volunteers often moves the right people to action.

Third, providing a trial service opportunity usually helps people who are on the fence about serving jump right in. Many potential volunteers are sidelined by fear of doing or saying the wrong thing. By providing an avenue for real relationships to start, you can help volunteers overcome their initial fear and develop a love for the special needs community. Your church's special events, such as respite events, moms' morning out, celebration meals, carnivals and holiday celebrations, are just a few ways for volunteers to provide two to three hours of service with low commitment but high impact to your ministry.

Fourth, do not underestimate the value of involving youth in your ministry. Teens and college students are often stellar buddies for several reasons.

Many students have grown up experiencing inclusion in their school settings and are often familiar with people with various special needs. Youth have a habit of assuming the best about a person with special needs; they rarely overprotect or coddle. Instead, they believe their friends can do many things and naturally encourage them to do so. Youth also seem to have a natural ability to adapt curriculum and activities to accommodate friends–an ability that is very useful in buddy ministry. Finally, they bring energy that is hard to engineer in more mature volunteers.

Training Buddies

Recruiting volunteers is one thing; keeping them is an entirely different subject. The first step to keeping great volunteers is to provide adequate training. Everyone who touches the life of a family with a member with special needs should have basic disability awareness and etiquette training; this includes buddies, greeters, ushers, pastoral staff, lead teachers, small-group leaders, and assistants.

Beyond this basic training, buddies and ministry leaders need training in church-wide policies and procedures, including toileting procedures, emergency medical procedures, evacuation plans, and chain of communication. These are items that are not unique to buddy ministry and should be communicated to volunteers in any ministry. Also, training your ministry team in the area of behavior modification is highly recommended.

Buddies will also benefit from training in their specific assignment; reading a simple fact sheet on their friend's diagnosis, talking through the completed intake form with the ministry leader and/or parents, and establishing a behavior management and discipleship plan are all helpful ways to prepare a buddy for service. Becoming acquainted with ministry resources like sensory bags, visual schedules, and tactile or electronic learning aids can also be helpful. Ultimately, the best training is hands-on. Having a new buddy shadow a veteran buddy is an excellent way to quickly communicate what is expected and how to accomplish it.

Sometimes considering what a buddy is not helps solidify what a buddy truly is. Jan Joaquin, a local disability ministry leader, says it this way, "A buddy is . . .

- A friend, not a babysitter.
- A role model, not a lead teacher.

- A partner, not a parent.
- An advocate, not an agent."

Walking potential buddies through these distinctions can ease anxiety for your volunteers and prevent the need to constantly retrain volunteers who misunderstand their role.

Pairing Buddies with Friends

Pray carefully through the potential partnerships that you can create through buddies and their friends. Is the friend very active and prone to running? Do not pair him with a senior buddy who has difficulty moving from place to place and who craves quiet. Instead, consider an active young adult who will not mind wearing his running shoes to church! Is the friend shy and withdrawn? Consider pairing that friend with a nurturing mother figure or with a strong, male role-model.

If possible, pair like genders together, particularly as friends age. A 15-year-old boy who is working hard at participating in youth group would probably appreciate having an older and wiser guy as his buddy rather than a grandmotherly figure. The younger the friend, the less this matters.

Take the age difference between buddy and friend into consideration when pairing as well. Youth, even those in middle school, can be very successful buddies. They can serve effectively in two ways: (1) as a peer buddy with adult oversight so that they do not have responsibility for managing their friend's behavior, or (2) as the sole buddy for a much younger child. Older teens can effectively serve older children. Young adults can effectively serve teens. Peer buddies can be highly successful at all ages with the proper adult support.

When a Diagnosis Is Suspected

Church leaders consistently ask how to handle a child who disrupts the class, preventing other students from learning. A child can be a distraction through over-participating: talking constantly, interrupting, not respecting another's personal space, or destroying property. Conversely, a child can be a distraction by not participating at all: leaving the learning environment, melting down, hiding, playing independently, not communicating, or becoming defiant. While you and your team may question if a disruptive child has special needs, it is not appropriate to assume the child does or to attempt to diagnose the child. Instead, consider the underlying motivation for any ministry: sharing the gospel and discipleship.

Once your leadership team and buddies have received some behavior modification training, they can begin to work with a child who has disruptive tendencies by considering the SEAT behavior functions addressed in the "What Buddies Provide" section of this book. As you attempt to work with the child through behavior modification, you can also consider two other valid options to address the situation: First, if you have a positive working relationship with the parent(s) and a good grasp of the situation in the classroom, sit down for an in-depth conversation on how you can better serve their child during the scheduled programming. The key is to take responsibility for the perceived problem instead of blaming the child or the parents. Ask questions such as "How can we adapt to better engage your child?" or "What does your child enjoy and not enjoy about our programming?" This provides the platform for productive collaboration. While brainstorming, offer the assistance of the buddy ministry if you feel that is the right fit.

Second, for families you may not initially feel comfortable talking with, or if you feel you need more information, gather some data. If a trusted buddy is available, assign one to the classroom as an aid for a few weeks, with the understanding that she will focus her attention on appropriately engaging the student in question. Do this from a positive perspective—you are looking for positive data to share with parents that having a buddy is a benefit to their child, not documenting every problem that arises to prove the child needs a buddy. If buddies are not available, or if you want more information, you may consider personally observing the class for a few consecutive sessions to document behaviors. In particular, you might want to answer the following questions:

- Is this student hearing and understanding the gospel teaching?
- Is this student able to engage in positive peer relationships?
- Does the lead teacher only use teaching techniques that reach students who are naturally quiet, calm, self-possessed, and still?
- Is there an unaddressed sensory issue or relational issue that is preventing appropriate

participation? (This could be over-stimulating music, games, lights or smells. It could be a subtle bullying relationship that causes social anxiety.)
- Does the student arrive with disruptive behaviors/attitudes? If so, do these behaviors appear after being dropped off, or do they manifest at a consistent point during the programming?

Once you feel you have an accurate understanding of the situation, sit down with the lead teacher and share your observations and insights. Perhaps handling transitions differently or changing where the student sits will make a big difference. Maybe allowing unconventional learning postures, such as pacing on the side of the room, lying on the floor in a designated space, or sitting under a table, will enable the student to focus. The student might simply need to hold something to keep his hands from wandering. Try these simple environmental fixes first, still using the buddy aid in the classroom if possible.

If you have addressed the environmental factors that are appropriate and you believe a buddy would still benefit the student, seek out the parents for a personal conversation. Regardless of the reason, if a diagnosis is not indicated on an intake form but there is a real need for extra support in the classroom, approach the parents with humility and grace. The conversation should center on helping you gain a better understanding on how to best include their child so that the child can hear and understand the gospel. Your goal ought to be seeing their child grow in faith, fellowship and service, not on taking a stab at diagnosing their child.

As a side note, typical classmates may want to engage in these unconventional learning supports even though they can participate well without them. If you believe that students will build better community and still receive the gospel and discipleship, then let them engage! If you know that utilizing these supports would actually distract them from learning well, explain that when they need support, you will be sure to provide it exactly the way they need it to learn the way God designed them to learn. Often a quick explanation and reassurance that you care equally for each class member are all that is needed. For in-depth help on integrating friends with special needs and their accommodations effectively, read Barbara Newman's *Helping Children Include Children with Disabilities*.

Working with Family Volunteers

While it may seem at first that any warm body will be a helpful addition to your growing buddy ministry, please take the time to truly screen your volunteers and make sure they are appropriately plugged into service. As previously noted, safety is of utmost importance in special needs ministry. Background checks should be required for any volunteer over 18 years of age, and references are a smart requirement for buddies of any age. Many churches have an application process already in place for their ministry volunteers. Your ministry should follow the pre-established policy of your church for screening volunteers, or work with leadership to create one if your church does not currently have one. This simple process can help ensure all due diligence is completed and paperwork is in order. It also communicates to potential volunteers that your ministry requires commitment and consistency. If a person applies to be a buddy but is clearly incapable of fulfilling the role, consider other ways they might serve, such as helping keep the files up to date, writing notes of encouragement to families and volunteers, or keeping sensory items clean and organized.

Often, family members of the friend you are serving will volunteer to serve in your ministry. Understanding their underlying motivation for volunteering is key to plugging them in correctly. A great general practice is to restrict family members from serving their own family member.

Parents will often volunteer their typical child to serve as their sibling's buddy, believing that since they know their brother or sister well, they are the best fit. Sometimes typical siblings volunteer on their own because they naturally feel the burden of responsibility and may not have learned how to interact with peers outside of that caregiver role. This is an opportunity to serve the entire family. Make a hard and fast rule that siblings do not buddy with siblings. If you can, go one step further and keep them from serving a friend in the same classroom, as they will often unconsciously take on their caregiver role with their sibling if they are in the same vicinity.

Parents may also volunteer to serve in your ministry for a variety of reasons. Many want to give back because they feel guilty about receiving such an incredible service. Here is an opportunity to help them discover other ways to give back to the body of Christ without feeling compelled to be a constant caregiver. Perhaps they are musically gifted and would enjoy joining the praise team or choir; take time to help them see the benefit of serving in this capacity, both for themselves and for their child. Serving as their child's buddy may limit the friendships their child with special needs builds with unrelated buddies.

Other parents are gifted in special needs ministry and volunteer out of a sincere, loving heart. Stick to your rule that immediate family members do not buddy together, and let them serve! You will know fairly quickly if they are serving for the right motivation.

Scheduling

A master schedule is an essential tool for an effective buddy ministry. Organized by the Buddy Ministry Coordinator or an appointed volunteer, this master calendar keeps track of when buddies are scheduled to serve with your ministry. Having people communicate when they expect to be available is critical in keeping a consistent, well-staffed ministry. Emergencies and illnesses will occur, but keeping a master calendar helps prevent holes.

An easy way to maintain the master calendar is to have volunteers communicate their known availability in advance, at least a month out, but three months out is ideal if you can get it. Doing this in advance helps buddies facilitate swapping weeks with their partner buddy and finding substitutes before they are absent. Establishing a calendar also communicates to your volunteers that their commitment to the ministry should be taken seriously. Whether or not their assigned friend attends Sunday school that morning they ought to be committed to serve. If their friend is not there, they can assist other friends or serve as a classroom aid.

Buddy Support

Providing ongoing personal support for the buddies in your ministry yields long-lasting results. Support can take the following forms, but certainly is only limited by your imagination:

- Praying for your buddies–I encourage you to pray that your buddies would have energy and wisdom as they serve and that they would also grow in their faith as they serve their friends.

- Encouraging your buddies–When you notice your buddies doing something well or going above and beyond, take time to thank them and let them know you appreciate them.
- Serving support–As your buddies serve their friends, make yourself or other leadership available to them to answer any questions that may arise. It can also be a good idea to check in with them individually every few months to make sure they have everything they need, troubleshoot any concerns, talk through new ideas, etc.
- Provide the right equipment–Having a bag, box, or bin of sensory items that buddies can use on an as-needed basis can make all the difference in their friends' participation. Similarly, having a designated space, such as a sensory room or a quiet corner, extends the learning environment options for a buddy and her friend. Useful for calming anxiety or meltdowns, these spaces can be used for a few moments as needed. However, if these spaces are required, be mindful to ensure that there are always two adults present when a friend is involved.
- Ongoing training–Holding trainings on various topics related to special needs ministry

throughout the year allows your buddies to grow in their knowledge and expertise as they continue serving their friends.

For a comprehensive look at recruiting, training and keeping great volunteers, check out *Engaging Game Changers* in the Irresistible Church collection.

Irresistible Conclusion

Nicole discovered the wonderful partnership of buddy ministry when she first volunteered at a Joni and Friends Family Retreat. At Family Retreat, individuals with disabilities are paired with a buddy throughout the week, allowing the whole family to rest and relax. Nicole was nervous about this new adventure, but she applied with several of her friends, thinking it would be fun to do together. The week before the retreat, all of Nicole's friends backed out—but Nicole went anyway.

When Nicole entered the teen program for the first time to meet her friend, she felt shy and uneasy. Nicole's assigned friend and another teen girl in a wheelchair were decorating the sidewalk with chalk. They called out to her, "Hey! Would you like to join us?" They made Nicole feel welcome by asking her questions and introducing her to friends. Over the next few days, Nicole came to love this group of teens and developed a profound respect for how they loved God and others.

That was several years ago. Since then, Nicole has not missed a single Family Retreat and even helps lead the teen program now. She has become a special needs elementary school teacher and sits on the board of a local special needs ministry. She has remained close friends with that original group of teens, and now when she has the opportunity to be a buddy to a person with special needs, she's not shy. You might hear her say, "Hey! Would you like to join me? I'd love to be your friend!"

What Nicole learned is that buddy ministry is the adaptor that allows the gospel to flow into the lives of special needs families, which allows them to plug into the greatest power source of all, Jesus, and His body, the church. If you travel, you know how frustrating it can be to have your phone or computer battery die simply because you did not have the right adaptor to plug it into the wall. Buddy ministry is that power adaptor for many families with special needs. A buddy partners with a person who may not fit directly into the existing programming. When paired together, they can be plugged into full capacity!

Throughout the pages of this book, we have examined the details of buddy ministry, including a biblical example, what buddies provide for church members with special needs, how to organize the ministry, and how to equip your volunteers. We have learned that buddy ministry is about more than just making a church service a viable option for caregivers who never seem to get a break. It is ultimately about making the life of your church accessible to all, and communicating how Christ and His kingdom accept all who come to Him in faith, regardless of their inherent abilities and disabilities.

When your church embraces this mentality, it will become irresistible. By that we mean that your church will be an authentic community built on the hope of Christ that compels people with disabilities to fully belong. When this happens, the world takes notice of our irresistible Savior who, through His redeeming work on the cross, now says to us, "Call Me Friend."

Becoming *Irresistible*

Luke 14 commands Christ followers to "Go quickly . . . find the blind, the lame, and the crippled . . . and compel them to come in!" While this sounds inspiring and daunting, exciting and overwhelming, motivating and frightening, all at the same time, what does it actually mean? How do we live and function within the church in such a way that families affected by disability are compelled to walk through our doors to experience the body of Christ?

We can certainly *compel* them by offering programs, ministries, events, and other church activities, but what if the compelling aspect was more about heart, culture, acceptance and embracing? What if our churches were overflowing with the hope of Jesus Christ . . . a hope not simply for those who "fit in" or look the part, but rather a hope to all, including the marginalized, downtrodden and outcast?

Becoming *Irresistible* is more than programs and activities—it is about a transformational work in our hearts . . . first as individuals and then as the body of Christ. *Irresistible* allows us to see each individual as he or she truly is: created in the image of God (Genesis 1:26-27), designed purposely as a masterpiece (Psalm 139:13-14), instilled with purpose, plans and dreams (Jeremiah 29:11), and a truly indispensable member of the kingdom of God (1 Corinthians 12:23). An *Irresistible Church* is an "authentic community built on the hope of Christ that compels people affected by disability to fully belong." It is powerful for a person to know that he or she is fully welcomed and belongs. *Irresistible* captures the heart of the church as it should be—how else do we explain the rapid growth and intense attraction to the church in the book of Acts? The heart of God was embodied through the people of God by the Spirit of God . . . and that is simply *Irresistible*!

The Irresistible Church Series is designed to help not only shape and transform the heart of the church, but also to provide the practical steps and activities to put *flesh* around the *heart* of the church—to help your church become a place for people to fully belong. Thank you for responding to the call to become *Irresistible.* It will not happen overnight, but it will happen. As with all good things, it requires patience and perseverance, determination and dedication, and ultimately an underlying trust in the faithfulness of God. May God bless you on this journey. Be assured that you are not alone—there are many on the path of *Irresistible.*

For more information or to join the community,
please visit www.irresistiblechurch.org.

Joni and Friends was established in 1979 by Joni Eareckson Tada, who at 17 was injured in a diving accident, leaving her a quadriplegic. Since its inception, Joni and Friends has been dedicated to extending the love and message of Christ to people who are affected by disability whether it is the disabled person, a family member, or friend. Our objective is to meet the physical, emotional, and spiritual needs of this group of people in practical ways.

Joni and Friends is committed to recruiting, training, and motivating new generations of people with disabilities to become leaders in their churches and communities. Today, the Joni and Friends International Disability Center serves as the administrative hub for an array of programs which provide outreach to thousands of families affected by disability around the globe. These include two radio programs, an award-winning television series, the Wheels for the World international wheelchair distribution ministry, Family Retreats which provide respite for those with disabilities and their families, Field Services to provide church training along with educational and inspirational resources at a local level, and the Christian Institute on Disability to establish a firm biblical worldview on disability-related issues.

From local neighborhoods to the far reaches of the world, Joni and Friends is striving to demonstrate to people affected by disability, in tangible ways, that God has not abandoned them–he is with them–providing love, hope, and eternal salvation.

Available Now in the Irresistible Church Series

Start with Hello

Introducing Your Church to Special Needs Ministry

Families with special needs often share that they desire two things in their church: accessibility and acceptance. Accessibility to existing structures, programs and people is an imperative. Acceptance with a sense of belonging by the others who also participate in the structures, programs and fellowship of the church is equally necessary. In this simple book you'll learn the five steps to becoming an accessible and accepting church.

To receive first notice of upcoming resources, including respite, inclusive worship and support groups, please contact us at churchrelations@joniandfriends.org.

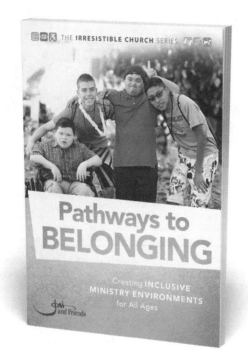

Other Recommended Resources

Beyond Suffering Bible

The *Beyond Suffering Bible* by Joni and Friends is the first study Bible made specifically for those who suffer and the people who love them. Uplifting insights from Joni Eareckson Tada and numerous experts and scholars who have experienced suffering in their own lives and will help you move beyond the "why" of suffering to grasp the eternal value God is building into our lives. Special features include: inspiring devotionals, biblical and contemporary profiles, Bible reading plans, connection points and disability ministry resources.

Find out more at http://www.joniandfriends.org/store/category/bibles/

Beyond Suffering® Student Edition

Beyond Suffering for the Next Generation: A Christian View on Disability Ministry will equip young people to consider the issues that affect people with disabilities and their families, and inspire them to action. Students who embrace this study will gain confidence to join a growing, worldwide movement that God is orchestrating to fulfill Luke 14:21-23: "Go out quickly into the streets and alleys of the town and bring in the poor, the crippled, the blind, and the lame.... so that my house will be full."

ISBN: 978-0-9838484-6-2
304 pages · 8.5″ x 11″
Includes CD-ROM

Joni: An Unforgettable Story

In this unforgettable autobiography, Joni reveals each step of her struggle to accept her disability and discover the meaning of her life. The hard-earned truths she discovers and the special ways God reveals his love are testimonies to faith's triumph over hardship and suffering. This new edition includes an afterword, in which Joni talks about the events that have occurred in her life since the book's original publication in 1976, including her marriage and the expansion of her worldwide ministry to families affected by disability.

ISBN: 978-0310240013
205 pages · Paperback

www.joniandfriends.org · P.O. Box 3333, Agoura Hills, CA 91376
(818) 707-5664 · Fax: (818) 707-2391 TTY: (818) 707-9707

Customizable Resources from the Book

Available for Download at

http://www.joniandfriends.org/church-relations/

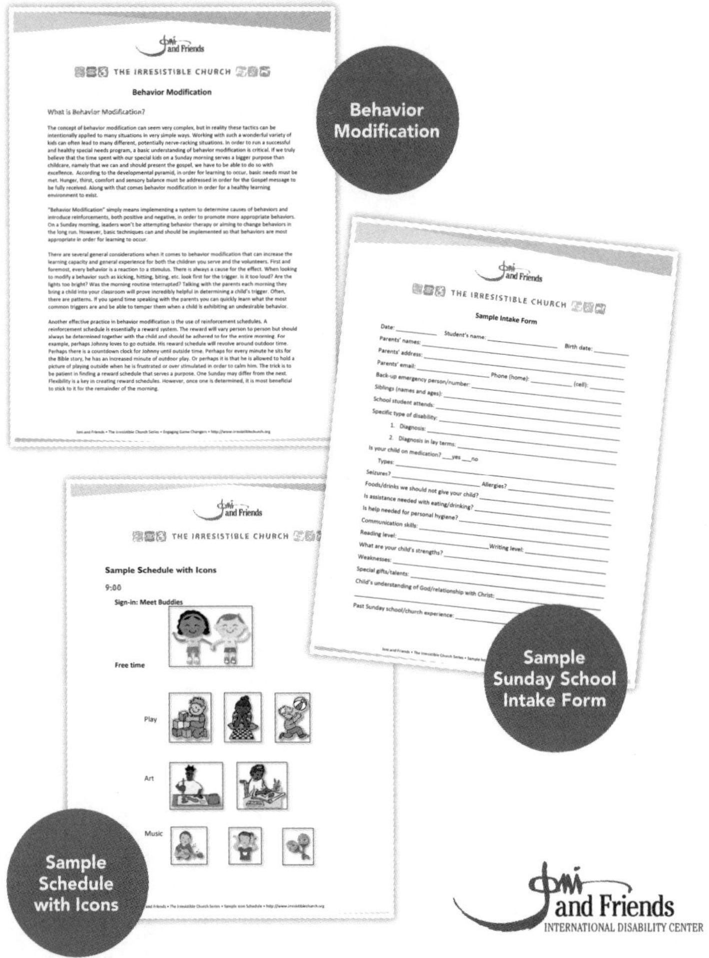

Joni and Friends

THE IRRESISTIBLE CHURCH

Behavior Modification

What is Behavior Modification?

The concept of behavior modification can seem very complex, but in reality these tactics can be intentionally applied to many situations in very simple ways. Working with such a wonderful variety of kids can often lead to many different, potentially nerve-racking situations. In order to run a successful and healthy special needs program, a basic understanding of behavior modification is critical. If we truly believe that the time spent with our special kids on a Sunday morning serves a bigger purpose than childcare, namely that we can and should present the gospel, we have to be able to do so with excellence. According to the developmental pyramid, in order for learning to occur, basic needs must be met. Hunger, thirst, comfort and sensory balance must be addressed in order for the Gospel message to be fully received. Along with that comes behavior modification in order for a healthy learning environment to exist.

"Behavior Modification" simply means implementing a system to determine causes of behaviors and introduce reinforcements, both positive and negative, in order to promote more appropriate behaviors. On a Sunday morning, leaders won't be attempting behavior therapy or aiming to change behaviors in the long run. However, basic techniques can and should be implemented so that behaviors are most appropriate in order for learning to occur.

There are several general considerations when it comes to behavior modification that can increase the learning capacity and general experience for both the children you serve and the volunteers. First and foremost, every behavior is a reaction to a stimulus. There is always a cause for the effect. When looking to modify a behavior such as kicking, hitting, biting, etc. look first for the trigger. Is it too loud? Are the lights too bright? Was the morning routine interrupted? Talking with the parents each morning they bring a child into your classroom will prove incredibly helpful in determining a child's trigger. Often, there are patterns. If you spend time speaking with the parents you can quickly learn what the most common triggers are and be able to temper them when a child is exhibiting an undesirable behavior.

Another effective practice in behavior modification is the use of reinforcement schedules. A reinforcement schedule is essentially a reward system. The reward will vary person to person but should always be determined together with the child and should be adhered to for the entire morning. For example, perhaps Johnny loves to go outside. His reward schedule will revolve around outdoor time. Perhaps there is a countdown clock for Johnny until outside time. Perhaps for every minute he sits for the Bible story, he has an increased minute of outdoor play. Or perhaps it is that he is allowed to hold a picture of playing outside when he is frustrated or over stimulated in order to calm him. The trick is to be patient in finding a reward schedule that serves a purpose. One Sunday may differ from the next. Flexibility is a key in creating reward schedules. However, once one is determined, it is most beneficial to stick to it for the remainder of the morning.

Joni and Friends

THE IRRESISTIBLE CHURCH

Sample Intake Form

Date: ______ Student's name: ______ Birth date: ______

Parents' names: ______

Parents' address: ______

Parents' email: ______ Phone (home): ______ (cell): ______

Back-up emergency person/number: ______

Siblings (names and ages): ______

School student attends: ______

Specific type of disability: ______

1. Diagnosis: ______
2. Diagnosis in lay terms: ______

Is your child on medication? ___yes ___no

Types: ______

Seizures? ______ Allergies? ______

Foods/drinks we should not give your child? ______

Is assistance needed with eating/drinking? ______

Is help needed for personal hygiene? ______

Communication skills: ______

Reading level: ______ Writing level: ______

What are your child's strengths? ______

Weaknesses: ______

Special gifts/talents: ______

Child's understanding of God/relationship with Christ: ______

Past Sunday school/church experience: ______

Joni and Friends

THE IRRESISTIBLE CHURCH

Sample Schedule with Icons

9:00

Sign-in: Meet Buddies

Free time

Play

Art

Music